First American Paperback Edition 2001
by Kane/Miller Book Publishers
La Jolla, California

Originally published in Japan under the title *Minna Unchi*
by Fukuinkan Shoten, Publishers Inc, Tokyo, 1977

For information contact:
Kane Miller, A Division of EDC Publishing
P.O. Box 470663
Tulsa, OK 74147-0663
www.kanemiller.com
www.edcpub.com

Library of Congress Caralog Card Number 92-56760

Manufactured by Regent Publishing Services, Hong Kong
Printed July 2013 in Shenzhen, Guangdong, China
22 23 24 25

ISBN: 978-1-929132-14-0

Everyone Poops
By Taro Gomi

Translated by Amanda Mayer Stinchecum

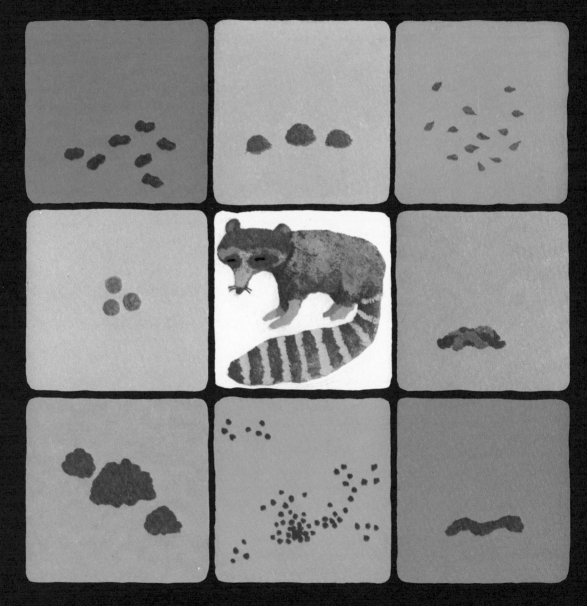

Kane Miller
A DIVISION OF EDC PUBLISHING

An elephant makes a big poop

A mouse makes a tiny poop

A one-hump camel makes a one-hump poop

And a two-hump camel makes a two-hump poop

Only kidding!

Fish poop

And so do birds

And bugs too

Different animals make different kinds of poop

Different shapes
Different colors
Even different smells

Which end
is the snake's behind?

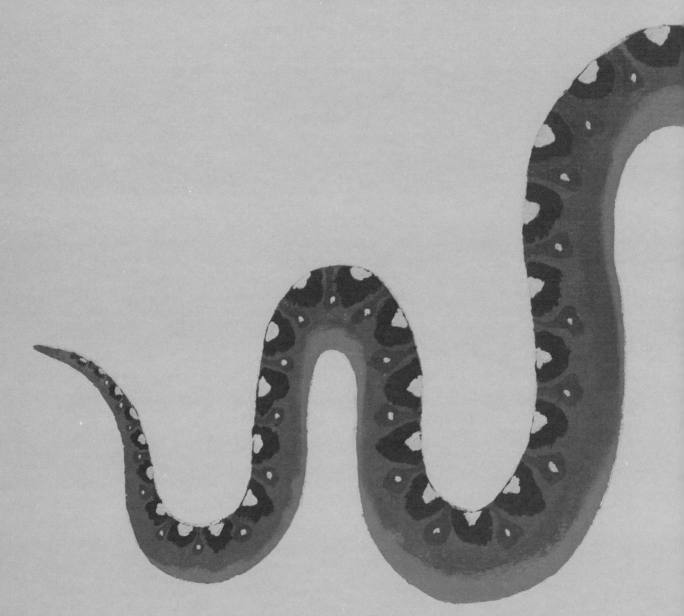

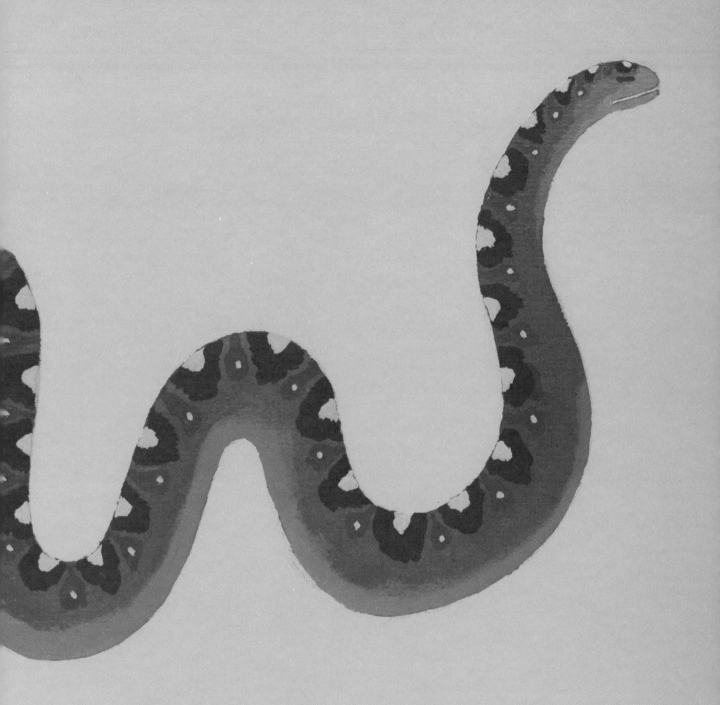

What does whale

poop look like?

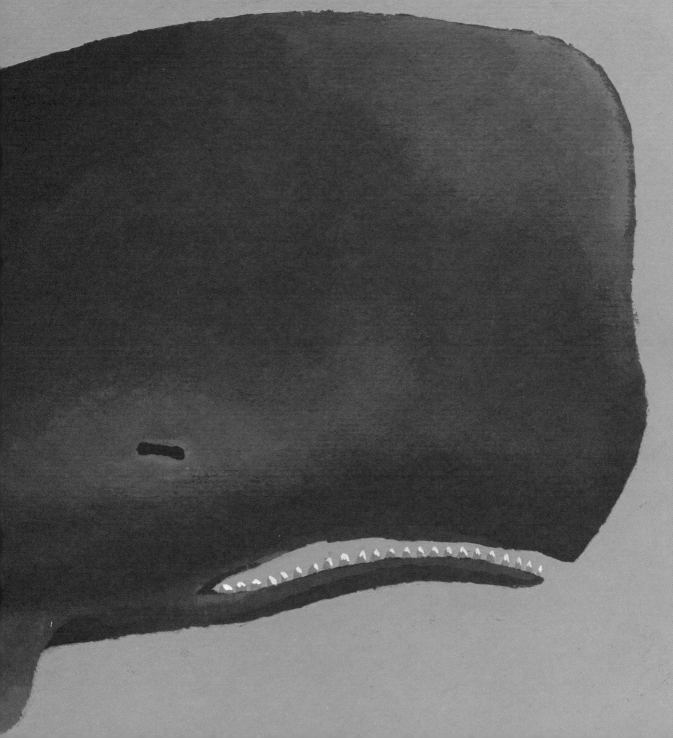

Some stop to poop

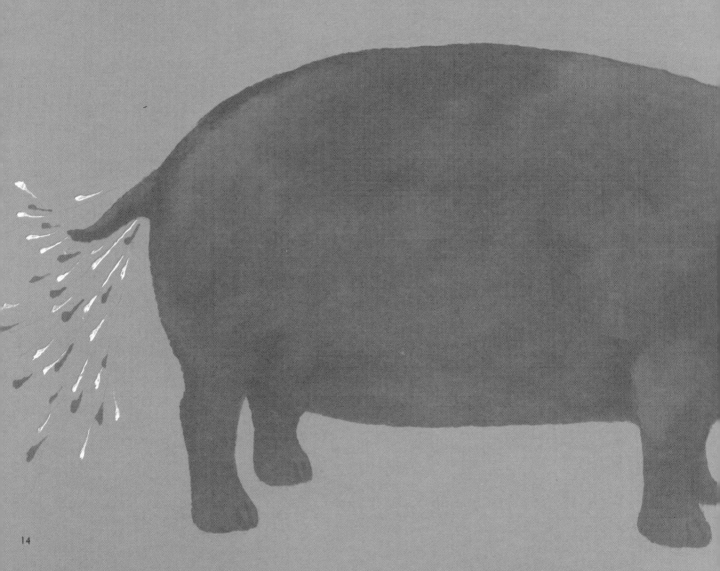

Others do it
on the move

Some poop here and there

Others do it in a special place

Grown-ups poop

Children poop too

While some children poop on the potty

Others poop in their diapers

Some animals poop
and pay no attention

Others clean up
after themselves

These poop by the water

This one does it in the water

He wipes himself
with paper,

then
flushes
it down

23

24

All living things eat, so

Everyone Poops

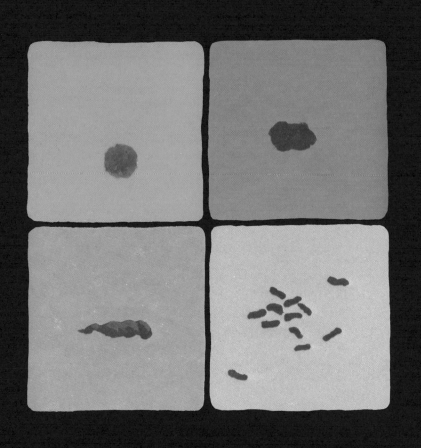